A SPIRIT DAUGHTER WORKBOOK

WRITTEN BY
JILL WINTERSTEEN

FOR THE FULL MOON
FRIDAY, NOVEMBER 15TH
1:29PM PT

WHY THE FULL MOON

For centuries, humans have stood in awe of the Full Moon. She is beautiful, mysterious, and magical. She also marks the halfway point from one New Moon to another. Just as the Sun helps us keep track of the hours in a day, the Moon helps us track the days of the Lunar Cycle. The Moon and her phases are just as predictable as the Sun, once we learn her rhythm. At the start of the Lunar Cycle, marked by the darkness of the New Moon, the Sun and Moon are together in the sky. They rise together, they set together. They are in sync, and so is their energy.

WHY THE FULL MOON

After the New Moon, the Moon begins to rise later and later each day. She also begins to make her journey around the Earth, no longer aligning with the Sun. We can watch this dance of Sun and Moon reflected in her growing crescent light. Once we see a Half Moon, we know she has made her way one quarter around the Earth, which is why this phase is called the First Quarter. At this point, the Moon is rising around midday and staying in our sky until midnight. The presence of the Half Moon in our early night sky signals that we are building light towards Full. During this phase, we are also building momentum with our dreams.

The Moon continues her journey around the Earth one more quarter until she reaches the halfway point of her orbit; the Full Moon. By this point, she is rising at the same time the Sun sets, and stays in our sky throughout the entire night, setting when the Sun rises. During this phase, the Moon stands in complete opposition to the Sun, allowing her to appear fully illuminated by the Sun's rays. She technically is only half-illuminated, as the other side of her is dark, but we can't see this from our vantage point. If we happened to be in space, on the other side of the Moon, she would look like a New Moon. For our purposes on Earth, though, a Full Moon opposes the Sun and lights up our night sky, marking the peak of the Lunar Cycle.

After the Full Moon, she continues to rise later and later as she completes her trip around the Earth. About a week after the Full Moon, she makes it yet another quarter (that's three now) appearing as our second Half Moon of the Lunar cycle, otherwise known as the Last Quarter Moon. This phase differs from the First Quarter because the Moon is losing light, or waning instead of waxing. She also waits until midnight to rise and sets midday. If you find yourself staring at a Half Moon in the early morning hours, it's the Waning Quarter, meaning we are about to encounter another New Moon soon. Waning Moons are times of release and preparation for the next Lunar Cycle.

Finally, the Moon completes her circle and meets with the Sun once again for the New Moon. She repeats this cycle every 29.5 days, cycling through the entire zodiac on her way, spending about 2.5 days in each zodiac sign. When the Moon and Sun are together for the New Moon, they share a zodiac sign and both highlight that energy. When the Moon is full, though, they are positioned in opposing zodiac signs, allowing these energies to confront one another. During a Full Moon, there is an opportunity for us to align with both the energies of Sun and Moon to integrate them within ourselves. This integration occurs after we become aware of the full spectrum of vibrations each Full Moon brings us.

This workbook is a journey through the opposing energies of Sun and Moon. By building awareness of the energy available during each Full Moon, we can form a balance point where the energies merge harmoniously, and allow us to break through the opposition to a new vibration. This breakthrough takes some work on our part, but the process is a perfect reflection of the Lunar cycle. The New Moon is our time to dream and create our visions; the Full Moon is our time to do the work necessary to manifest them. Luckily, we have a predictable clock in our sky letting us know which opportunities for growth to direct our energy towards each month.

TAURUS FULL MOON

The Taurus Full Moon is an invitation to come home to ourselves. Taurus is ruled by Venus and teaches us that our earthly existence is nothing short of a miracle. We are beautiful in every way, as is our life's journey. This Moon directs our attention to our bodies and our embodiment of energy in this lifetime. It's an opportunity to be present with all our senses, to feel our feet on the ground, and gaze at the wonders above us.

TAURUS FULL MOON

Ruled by the Earth element, this Full Moon provides a stable container amidst the emotional rollercoaster of Scorpio Season. Taurus reminds us that no matter how chaotic life can feel within or around us, we always have resources to support us. Some of these resources may be well-defined tools of emotional regulation. Some may be techniques that connect us to our body and breath, like yoga or meditation. Some may be the support of a friend or larger community.

As you work with the energy of this Full Moon, feel the stability within and around you. Remind yourself that you can always rely on yourself. You can face any storm and find the center. Furthermore, you can use the storm to evolve and find the next version of yourself. You have inner resources that can be called upon anytime you need them. You have yourself.

Feel the container this Full Moon provides. It's like a warm hug that lets you know everything is going to be alright. If available, find some time to stand under the light of the Moon this day and feel the stillness available to you. When the Taurus Full Moon is high in the sky, everything else becomes quiet. It feels like Earth itself takes a pause, and after that pause, there is a wave of relief. Lean into this feeling today and let it return you home.

Then feel how this home was with you all along. Even when the world throws you about and you feel like you're falling through the sky, you always have a foundation to land upon within yourself. You are your own rock, and you have everything you need to manifest your greatest potential. You are your own foundation. Feel this strength within you this Moon and release anything that makes you doubt it.

Understanding that you are your own home, and you possess all the tools you'll ever need to build the life you desire, enables you to venture into the unknown. The Taurus Full Moon is a time to feel your attachments to your comfort zones. These are the places which initially feel like they nurture you, but in fact actually prevent your growth.

Comfort zones can be people, places, or things. They show up in the form of jobs, romantic relationships, even cities. They block you from manifesting your potential and hold you back simply because they are familiar. The familiar is comfortable, and growth generally is not.

In order to leave your comfort zones to create, or take leaps of faith, you need inner reliance. You need to trust that you can always rely on yourself no matter which way the road turns. You must know with every fiber of your being that you are your greatest resource and you can always bring yourself back home.

As you make your way through the energy of this Full Moon, feel its power to bring you to the beauty of your soul. Let it illuminate your strength, your perseverance, and your power to create your life. Connect deeply with your body and senses to feel your way through this period of your life and let yourself bask in the present moment under the light of the Moon. Pause, find stillness, then dive deep into the unknown, releasing any fear that holds you back, knowing that you can always save yourself.

TAURUS MOON X SCORPIO SUN

On this Full Moon, we are working with the energies of Taurus and Scorpio, where the Moon and the Sun are positioned. Taurus and Scorpio form an axis of energy. Every astrological energy has a high side or low, shadow, side. During a Full Moon, the signs where the Moon and Sun are positioned are fully illuminated. We can feel all of their energies, which in part is what makes a Full Moon so intense.

A Full Moon grants us the opportunity to observe where and how we are embodying lower frequencies of the signs involved. Lower vibrations block us from manifesting our visions by causing misalignment with our souls. They cause our energy to stagnate and even move in circles as we repeat patterns in our lives unconsciously. By recognizing these lower vibrations, we can shift them through conscious awareness. We can break patterns that keep us trapped in a life that doesn't match our potential.

Looking at Scorpio and Taurus, we see two sides of the same coin. They are both concerned with the present moment. They both want to help us find stillness and center our energy. Scorpio does this by encouraging us to face all of our shadows, demons, and life cycles. As we wade through our trauma, fears, and pain, we can find our way to the bottom of it all. Here we find a thread that binds everything together. In feeling this interconnectedness of every energy, we find our truth, and we find stillness. Scorpio wants us to experience every up and down life has to offer and, at the end of this rollercoaster ride, we find peace.

Taurus, on the other hand, also wants us to find peace, but through connecting with tangible resources we can touch. Instead of digging through our shadows, Taurus encourages us to look outside ourselves to see our reflection in all of nature. It reminds us that we go through the same cycles as the seasons, carry the same energy as the ocean. Like a tree, we too can stand firm in the midst of any storm. It's not that Taurus wants us to ignore our emotions, but rather to go beyond them. Taurus asks us to seek comfort not through understanding our own energy but through understanding our place within the energy of the Universe. We are one with everything, and from this oneness, we can find stillness. Furthermore, this stillness brings out our most creative self, which is also connected to the creativity of the Universe.

The lower frequencies of Scorpio show up when we find ourselves in a constant loop of transformation. In this frequency, we never feel good enough and are always looking for ways to improve upon ourselves. We become attached, even addicted, to creating events that pressure us to evolve. We may even attract the same type of person over and over again because they cause the same cycle of drama in our lives. Although we may be trying to heal from these cycles, we miss the opportunity to break out of them through positive transformation. Instead, we keep riding the roller coaster. In the lower side of Scorpio, we can become obsessed with the darkness in life and focus too heavily on what we, and others, need to change instead of appreciating the positive energies of life.

If you find yourself aligning with the lower vibrations of Scorpio, pause amid all the transforming to appreciate where you have been and who you have been. Love every version of yourself and reflect on the journey of your life. Then ground into the present moment and be still for a while. Give yourself permission to be who you are right now without feeling the need to work on anything. Pause between the cycles of your life and honor the person you are today.

The lower frequencies of Taurus cause us to look outside ourselves to tangible resources, but not those of nature. Instead of feeling connected with all of nature, we constantly need to gather more possessions, time, and money. We feel anxious about what we lack in our lives and never feel we have enough

TAURUS MOON X SCORPIO SUN

to feel centered. We may become preoccupied with the number in our bank account or the packages arriving at our door. We may even become addicted to tangible manifestations of nature, like comforting food and luxury items we can't quite afford. This vibration of Taurus makes us forget about our connection with nature. It makes us feel unsupported. In an effort to find support, we seek physical comfort.

The lower vibration of Taurus also makes us feel insecure. It causes us to forget about inner resilience and fools us into thinking we need to rely on forces outside ourselves. If the high side of Taurus teaches us that we are the strength of nature, the low side causes us to forget about our universal connection, and makes us question our very existence. This lower vibration also causes us to worry excessively about money and abundance. It causes us to forget that we are infinitely abundant in all energies and instead encourages us to focus on lack. Instead of holding the simple truth that we are abundant beings, this low side compels us to overcomplicate things. It makes us question how we are creating abundance and if we are even worthy of it in the first place.

If you find yourself aligning with the lower, or shadow, side of Taurus, observe the behaviors that it causes. Do you find yourself checking your bank account too often? Do you feel insecure about your place in the world? Do you not feel worthy of the abundance that is your birthright? And are you complicating your life by looking too far outside yourself for answers that rest in the stillness of your energy?

Become aware of how these lower frequencies of Taurus show up in your life and accept that they are part of you. They deserve compassion and acknowledgment. Then give yourself more time to sit with your feelings about these energies and your observations. Feel the stillness within you. Feel your connection with nature and your part in the vast Universe. Breathe deep and know that the Earth is supporting you, and trust your life course. Trust your ability to rely on yourself. You can survive any storm, and you don't even have to know it's coming. Let go of the need to project the future to control it. Instead, feel your stillness, resilience, and ability to feel creative solutions when needed. Your instinct is strong. Resist the urge to overcomplicate or overanalyze it because it makes you feel more in control of the world around you. Instead, look for the simple connections that remind you of your strength.

As you work with the lower vibrations of both Taurus and Scorpio, notice where repeating patterns are showing up in your life. Make different choices that break the ongoing loops you feel trapped by. Become aware of how your choices, even the energetic ones, create the cycles of your life. Ask yourself if you choose certain patterns and even people because they keep you in a familiar cycle of drama, without which you would feel lost. Or look at your cycles with finances and abundance and ask if they are keeping you in an infinite loop of insecurity.

Breaking patterns can cause you to feel insecure. This Full Moon is here to help you break through old foundations that cause drama and insecurity in your life. As you crack your old self open, you may feel vulnerable for a time until you establish a new foundation and way of being. As you go through this transformation, feel your inner strength, choose the path of the unknown, and find freedom from perpetual cycles that bind you.

When you shift from the lower vibrations of both Scorpio and Taurus and into the higher vibrations, find yourself in the present moment, full of inner resilience, and capable of creating any life you desire.

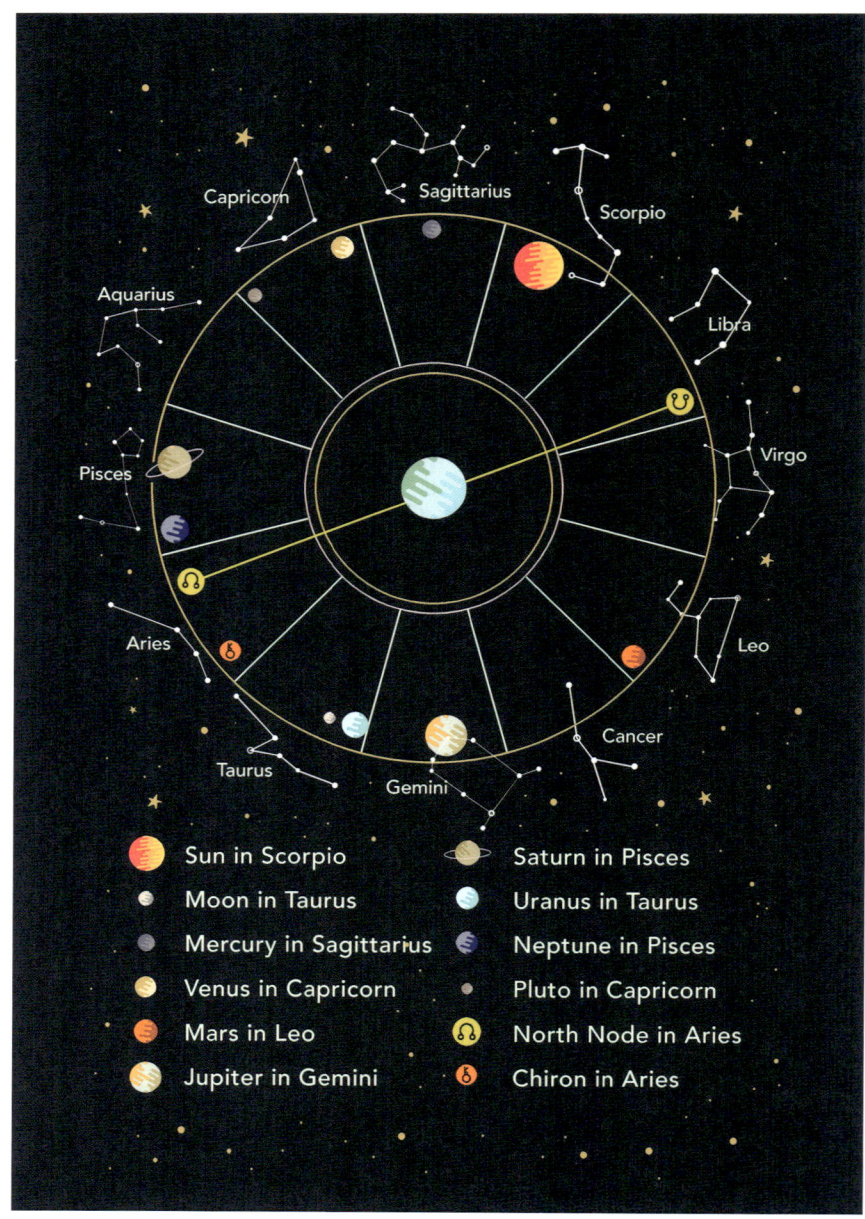

Sun in Scorpio
Moon in Taurus
Mercury in Sagittarius
Venus in Capricorn
Mars in Leo
Jupiter in Gemini

Saturn in Pisces
Uranus in Taurus
Neptune in Pisces
Pluto in Capricorn
North Node in Aries
Chiron in Aries

ASPECTS

We have quite a few aspects this Full Moon adding to the energy of the day. The most influential aspect is a conjunction between the Moon and Uranus Retrograde in Taurus. When cosmic bodies are conjunct, their energies enhance one another.

Uranus is the planet of change and movement. It tends to cause earthquakes, some minor, some major. Uranus influences the collective energy and helps us move forward as a society. Uranus is positioned in Taurus until 2026 and takes us on a journey of reconnecting with the Earth. In true Uranus fashion, it is calling attention to ways we as a collective need to nourish the planet we live on. Uranus's methods are not subtle, but ultimately its placement in Taurus will help us form a new connection with the Earth, ideally one that respects femininity and al beings equally.

On a personal level, Uranus breaks things up, including our attachments, so that we can build anew. Its conjunction with the Moon, which rules our emotional body, al ows us to break free of longstanding emotional patterns that are ruling us.

Uranus is one of two planets that rotate in the opposite direction compared to the other planets. It is also the only one that appears to roll instead of spin. Uranus teaches us that sometimes we need to go completely in the opposing direction of our usual pattern to create real change in our lives.

It also teaches us to go against the grain of society and what we were taught, challenging the habits we unconsciously have picked up from those around us. Many emotions that rule our energetic body are merely habits we formed. They are reactions we learned as children and may not even reflect our true selves. On this Full Moon, feel into the emotions that govern your world. Ask yourself what their origin is, and then challenge yourself to shake them up. Envision different reactions ard different ways you could feel.

While the Moon is conjunct Uranus, the Sun is forming an exact opposition with it. Oppositions can cause tension, which then leads to breakthroughs. The Sun governs our core personality and often symbolizes what holds us together. Uranus opposing the Sun challenges the very foundation of who we are. It asks us to dissolve our identity and feel into our deepest truth.

This Full Moon is a reminder that we are energy in our simplest form, and that energy is connected to all of nature and the Universe. We often cling to labels, definitions, and titles to validate our existence. On this Full Moon, feel the grounding energy Taurus provides, and let that stability support you as you break free of every attachment. Liberate yourself from things that limit your expansion ard know you are infinite. Your possibility is boundless.

FULL MOON HOROSCOPES

ARIES RISING

This Full Moon lights up your second house of finances and your wallet might be in for a few surprises. It's smart to think back to the days around May 7th, when you might've just begun ideating the things coming full circle now. Notice how your values have shifted over the past six months, and if there's anything you need to release in order to better align with your committed partnerships. Power struggles could also be surfacing now, so prioritize freedom in any discussions around finances.

TAURUS RISING

This Full Moon lights up your first house of self. Like it or not, you're being asked to change and this moment is putting that initiation on full display. Think back to May 7th and any seeds you may have planted back then for some clues as to what is reaching culmination now. You might not be a huge fan of surprises, but if any power struggles have been brought to light...standing in your truth will surprise others. Don't back down from what you need to be authentically you.

GEMINI RISING

This Full Moon lights up your twelfth house of surrender. Whether you enjoy spending time alone or not is less important than the value it has to offer you right now. If you can find time to get still, your subconscious is ready to send shockwaves of inspiration your way. Prioritize behind the scenes work around this lunation and trust that what you're doing will become more visible right on time. May 7th, the corresponding New Moon, might have some clues as to what your subconscious is whispering now. Pay attention.

CANCER RISING

This Full Moon lights up your eleventh house of community and might come with a few twists and turns within your circles. If you have a friend with a bright idea, don't hesitate to listen and see where it goes. You likely seeded something back in early May that connects with what's unfolding within your community now. If you've been facing any power struggles in your one on one connections, now is the time to stand your ground. If your authentic truth upsets people, so bet it.

LEO RISING

This Full Moon lights up your tenth house of public reputation and it's a loud moment for you and your audience! The stars might have finally aligned on a project you've been working to get off the ground— as this lunation is full of the recognition you've been manifesting. Thinking back to May 7th and what you were seeking at that time might make the happenings unfolding now less surprising. If power struggles have been part of any work dynamics...now is the time to speak your truth.

FULL MOON HOROSCOPES

VIRGO RISING

This Full Moon lights up your ninth house of higher beliefs and you might surprise yourself with how you're viewing the world around you. Since May 7th, the corresponding New Moon in Taurus, you've been exploring the word around you in entirely new ways. Whether you're physically traveling or moving through the astral realms, your beliefs are evolving. If the new ways you're viewing the world have transformed your wellness routines, you're right on track.

LIBRA RISING

This Full Moon lights up your eighth house of transformation...and there's nothing light-hearted about it. You're likely in a major moment of transition and might be contemplating a surprising collaboration. If you're unsure of the work to be done– think back to the corresponding Taurus New Moon on May 7th.

FULL MOON HOROSCOPES

Think about the resources you were sharing with others around that time, and ask yourself if your needs are now being met. If not, now is the moment to speak your truth authentically.

SCORPIO RISING

This Full Moon lights up your seventh house of committed partnerships and, as ever, there could be more surprises in store for this area of your life. Be on the lookout for chance encounters and people that make you stop and think. Think back to what you were manifesting within your serious relationships back on May 7th, and notice if any of those wishes are culminating now. You might have also been facing some power struggles in your career recently. If that's influencing your partnerships, now is the time to claim your freedom.

SAGITTARIUS RISING

This Full Moon lights up your sixth house of daily routines and something might be catching you off guard. This could equally play out like a lightbulb moment surrounding your habits and help you revolutionize the way you're accomplishing tasks. Likely, since May 7th, it's been clear that something's needed to change in this area of your life. You might be receiving answers to questions that you initiated back at that New Moon. If you've experienced any push and pull with the help you're receiving (or not) in your rituals, now is the time to speak up.

CAPRICORN RISING

This Full Moon lights up your fifth house of romance and creativity and likely offers some surprising news when it comes to children in your life...and/or your own inner child! This lunation wants you to connect with your playful side in an entirely new way. If you're unsure what that looks like, think back to what you were wishing for around the corresponding New Moon on May 7th. And if any power struggles have been unfolding in your relationship dynamics because of this quest for more play– now is the time to address them.

AQUARIUS RISING

This Full Moon lights up your fourth house of home and family and it's become clear that something has to change. Whether it's time to move to a new city or you're doing some major renovations, this moment is all about progress...even if it's hard. Think back to what you were dreaming of creating in the world around the corresponding New Moon on May 7th. If your root systems haven't morphed into that ideal yet, it might be time for some radical changes on the home front.

PISCES RISING

This Full Moon lights up your third house of communication and you might be ready to speak your truth in a newfound way. You typically are the peacekeeper around town, but this lunation is no time to shy away from engaging in a way that pushes the boundaries of your local community. Think back to what you were talking about back in early May, when we experienced the corresponding New Moon. Notice if you've met more people that challenge your perspectives since then– or if you still need to travel and seek them out.

TAURUS LUNAR FLOW

Taurus rules the throat, neck, thyroid gland, and vocal tract. This eclipse is a time to become grounded in your body, and from that foundation, open to the beauty of your expression. Move slowly through the following sequence. Challenge yourself to deepen both your inhale and exhale in every pose and feel the quiet stillness of your body as it aligns with the Earth energy.

SEATED SIDE BEND

Start in a seated, cross-legged position. Sit tall with your spine straight and, if you need to, place a blanket underneath your hips to prop them up higher than your knees. Inhale and lift your right arm to the ceiling. Exhale, side bend over the left, placing your left hand about a foot away from your left hip. Reach your right arm in line with your ear, palm facing down, fingertips reaching. Relax through your neck, allowing your left ear to fall to your left shoulder, stretching the right side of your neck. Breathe here for 5 breaths as you release the tension in your neck. Slowly come upright, then switch sides.

WARRIOR 2

Step your feet apart 3 to 4 feet wide on your mat, facing the side of the room. Turn your left foot toward the back of the mat and angle your right foot to 45 degrees. Bend in your front knee and reach your arms out to either side for Warrior 2. Reach actively through your fingertips. Feel the strength of your legs supporting you and ground down into the Earth. Breathe here for 5 breaths, then switch sides.

* Visit spiritdaughter.com/collections/zodiac-yoga to flow with our Taurus Zodiac Yoga video.

TAURUS LUNAR FLOW

GODDESS POSE

Bring both feet back to parallel, then turn them out at a 45-degree angle. Bend into your knees, lining them up with your third toe. Draw your lower belly in, tilting your tailbone to the floor. Bend your elbows at your side ribs and face your palms up to the sky in a receptive position. Take 5 to 10 breaths here, feeling your hips—your seat of creativity—open to the potential held within them.

LIZARD POSE

Come to hands and knees on the ground. Step your left foot to the outside of your left hand and stretch your right leg back on the ground, keeping your knee on the floor. Both hands should be on the inside of your left foot. Sink your hips forward and down. If able, come down onto your elbows or stay on your hands. Allow your left knee to fall open to the side as you breathe deeply into your hips. Stay here for one minute, then switch sides.

BRIDGE POSE

Lie on your back with your knees bent, feet hips width apart. Your feet should be close enough to your hips that you can gently brush your heels with your fingertips. On inhale, lift your hips, keeping your knees in line with your ankles. Shimmy your shoulders underneath you slightly so that you can grasp your hands. Press down into your upper arms to help lift your chest higher. Breathe deeply into your lungs on each inhale. On exhale, lift a little higher in your hips. Stay here for 5 breaths before releasing.

CAMEL POSE

Come to kneeling with your hips over your knees. Place your hands on your low back for support. Inhale, reach your chest to the sky, lengthening out your spine. As you exhale, slowly bend backward, keeping your back supported and your hips over your knees. On each inhale, reach through your chest. On each exhale, bend back a bit more. If it's comfortable, let your head fall back, opening your neck and your expression. Breathe deeply for 5 breaths, then return to kneeling. Sit back on your heels and observe your breath and the openness of your heart.

SUPINE TWIST

Lie on your back. Hug your left knee into your chest, then twist to the right, with your left knee out to this side. Reach out your left arm and look to the left. Stay here for 5 breaths before switching sides. Feel your spine and neck open in this twist and feel supported by the floor beneath you.

SAVASANA

Release onto the floor, lying with your palms up and eyes closed. Feel grounded through your body, still in your mind, and free in your energy.

TAURUS MEDITATION

The Taurus Full Moon is an opportunity to align with the present moment. Meditation of any kind is the perfect pairing for this Moon. It allows us to drop into the moment as the mind quiets and we are left with the stillness of the present moment. The challenging part of any meditative practice is quieting the constant thoughts that race through our minds. The key is to allow these thoughts in but not become attached to them. See them as clouds drifting through the sky of your mind, coming in and leaving with no attention from you. This skill can take years to master, but it is one worth dedication and commitment. A still mind is the greatest gift of all, as it gives us a place to rest from the chaos of the world and our own emotions.

HEAR YOURSELF
The first step to finding stillness in the mind is hearing its many thoughts. Begin the meditation process by taking a piece of paper and writing down all of the thoughts that float into your mind constantly. These include all of your worries, fears, to-do lists, work agendas, and so on. Allow a continuous stream of consciousness to pour from your mind to the paper. Resist the urge to filter any of your thoughts. Just write them down. Consider this a form of purging your mind of the random thoughts that normally run wild. Take your time with this process, even pausing for moments to allow more thoughts to surface. Also, don't be concerned about the format, grammar, or even spelling. Just write, allowing your mind to empty, then go quiet.

SENSORY MEDITATION – 10 MINUTES
Wherever you find yourself, simply close your eyes and allow your body to relax. You can be seated, standing, or lying down. Allow in the sounds around you. Mentally drop the unconscious walls you have built to protect your concentration. Do not focus on any one sound. Allow your mind to travel from one sound to another. Resist the urge to label the sounds. It does not matter if it's a bird chirping or the hum of the heater. Observe the sound for what it is—merely a vibration. Keep your mind moving, not lingering on any one sound for too long. You'll find that the longer you do this meditation, the more sounds you will notice. This awareness is the point. You want to hear everything, even the subtle sounds, without labeling them. As you embrace the sounds around you, it will bring you more into the present moment and into your body.

MANTRA MEDITATION – 5 MINUTES
Mantras are short phrases we repeat to ourselves. We already carry many unconscious mantras, which pop into our minds throughout the day. Through repeating the mantras below, we replace the unconscious ones, which often work against us, with positive, uplifting ones capable of attracting a new vibration. On the Taurus Full Moon, repeat these phrases for five minutes, or longer if you desire, as a way of introducing new programing into your energetic field.

I am present.

I forgive myself.

I am focused on the now.

I am worthy.

I am ready.

Once you finish repeating them, bring your mind back to stillness and quiet. Feel your presence in the moment, for however long you can, while resting at peace in your mind and energy.

TAURUS CIRCLE SET-UP

On this Full Moon, we are working with the elements of Earth, from Taurus, Water, from Scorpio. Water and Earth together create mud, which is deeply detoxifying and fertile. These elements also create flowers. Feel how the coming together of water and earth open a pathway for clearing and beauty in your life. Align with all four elements when creating your space.

Choose a space that feels grounded and connected to Mother Earth, but expansive enough to provide a container for your evolution. You can practice outside close to the ground or choose a space that contains the Wood element. If these are not available to you, place plants and crystals in your circle to bring the Earth inside. You can also practice alone or in a community. It's entirely up to you.

Allow Earth to ground you, Air to inspire you, Water to cleanse you, and Fire to keep you motivated. You can represent all elements in your circle to bring these energies into your space. If possible, build a fire outside to represent that element. You can also light candles in your space. For Air, use auric sprays, feathers to fan the smoke from dried herb bundles, or an oil diffuser. Use crystals and flowers to represent the Earth element.

Crystals that align with the energy of Taurus are Jade, Pink Opal, Green Onyx, and Lepidolite. They will help ground your energy and connect you with the Earth. Crystals for Scorpio are Onyx, Shungite, Ruby Fushite, Hematite, and Tourminalated Quartz. These crystals will help you ride the waves of transformation with courage and provide you with protection. Flowers for Taurus and Scorpio include peonies, hibiscus, and geranium. Bring in the element of Water through a vase or a metal bowl containing water. Gather all of your supplies and build your circle.

| JADE | PINK OPAL | GREEN ONYX | LEPIDOLITE |

| TOURMINALATED QUARTZ | RUBY FUSHITE | HEMATITE | ONYX |

Create an outline with your objects, anchoring the four directions—North, South, East, and West—with either a crystal or candle. If you are creating an altar, set it up in the westerly part of the circle, as this direction helps energies release. Water is the element associated with the West and represents transition. This is the direction of the sunset, so it represents the ending of day and the beginning of night. By setting your altar here, you are ushering in energy to help you change and release. Your altar can include crystals, images, flowers, notes from your journal, or a poem. You can also place different talismans that symbolically represent where you have been and where you are going. Altars help provide a place for your intentions for this night. What do you want to call in? What do you want to release? Who are your guides? What will remind you of your purpose? Likewise, what will hold space and be a container for your work?

Once the perimeter is set, cleanse the area with a dried herb bundle, like rosemary or lavender. You can also use a space-clearing spray. Begin cleansing at the easterly pcint, moving to the South, West, North, then back to the East. As you cleanse the circle, imagine a white light encasing it, protecting it from any external energies. Before your guests enter, cleanse each one of them, then yourself. Once you have all entered the circle, pause for a moment to let the energy settle before you begin.

Follow your intuitive guidance when leading a circle. Begin by having members introduce themselves. Talk about the astrological energy of the day and how it is affecting each one of you. Share and learn from each other about your unique experiences with this Full Moon. Give plenty of space for each person to speak. Follow your conversation with the meditation practice in this book to calm the mind. You can then explore the rest of the practices. Practice the releasing ritual before going onto the questions. You can then conclude the circle with card pulling and statements of gratitude for yourself, one another, and the Universe.

TAURUS CARD READING

What energy will help me break through limiting patterns?	What energy will help me feel supported in my creativity?	What energy will help me slow down and feel my center?
+ CARD PULLED:	+ CARD PULLED:	+ CARD PULLED:

Reading Cards is a beautiful way to access your intuition and tap into your, and the Universe's, higher wisdom. Anyone can pull cards, as long as you are willing to receive the information they provide. You need no prior experience, or training, just an open and clear mind.

You may use any cards you like for this practice, including but not limited to: Tarot Cards, Animal Medicine Cards, Oracle Cards or any Affirmation Cards. You also can pull cards from a few decks to gain different perspectives. If you are new to card pulling, try to ask only one deck the same question, as asking different decks the same question can become quite confusing. Below are some general guidelines on how to pull cards. Please improvise as needed and above anything else, listen to your intuition.

CLEAR YOUR MIND
A settled, grounded mind is essential for pulling cards. The last thing you want is random thoughts running around when you are trying to receive clear answers from yourself. Practice the breath work and meditation in this workbook to prepare and settle your mind. You may also clear your mind using sound frequencies through singing bowls. These can either be crystal or metal bowls. Play the bowl, or bowls, for about 3-5 minutes to help rid your mind of external noise as you focus on the harmony of the sound.

TAURUS CARD READING

PICK YOUR DECK
There are many different decks out there. You can choose as many as you like. Know, though, that they each provide you a different energy or medicine. Tarot Cards are the most popular and should be used carefully. Although very useful, Tarot cards can give the wrong impression if you interpret them harshly. Animal Medicine cards offer different types of messages from the animal realm which can help align with the spirit of nature. These cards give you the medicine you need to apply to your situation or question. Affirmation cards provide you with guidance in the form of words or phrases. When reading these cards, it is best to meditate on what the affirmation means for you. It is also helpful to repeat the affirmation a few times and see how it makes you feel. There are many other cards you can experiment with, like Goddess Cards, Angel Cards, and so on. The important thing to remember with any card is that they each have different angles and sides. There are often a few interpretations of the same card.

SHUFFLE
Shuffle the cards the easiest way for you. Some cards are smaller and can be shuffled like a regular deck of playing cards, while others will take some effort. If all else fails, spread them out on the floor in front of you then regather them. Keep a clear mind while shuffling. You can also repeat " I am open to receiving guidance and intuition." Refrain from asking your questions until the next step.

TAURUS CARD QUESTIONS
You are free to ask the deck any questions you need answers to on this Full Moon. The following questions are meant to help you harness the energy of Taurus through the cards to clarify some of these energies in your mind. This is a three-part card reading, where you'll ask the deck three questions. Before beginning, spread your freshly shuffled cards in a wide arc in front of you. Use your left middle finger to choose the card, first waving your hand slowly over the cards. You'll feel a magnetic pull, or slight tingle, in your fingertip when you hover over the right card. Chose one card at a time, taking a moment to breathe in between questions. Keep the cards flipped over until you pull all three.

What energy will help me break through limiting patterns?

What energy will help me feel supported in my creativity?

What energy will help me slow down and feel my center?

TAKE THEM IN
Once you have your cards, flip them over. Before looking up their meaning, sit with them for a moment and allow them to speak to you. Intuit your own meaning and interpretation of the card. What is the card trying to tell you? What are you trying to tell yourself? After a few moments with the cards, look up their meaning. Sit with that information, merging it with your intuitive meaning of the cards.

As with everything, enjoy this process. Do not worry if you are doing it right or wrong. Just follow your intuition, and trust the journey. Accept the cards you are dealt and use their energy wisely to help guide you when you need it the most.

22

As uncomfortable as growth may be,

squeezing into spaces you've outgrown

is even more uncomfortable.

- spirit daughter

TAURUS PRACTICES

The Taurus Full Moon brings powerful energy for breaking through old patterns that hold us back. This is your chance to evolve and create positive change in your life. The following practice is designed to help you harness the energy of the Full Moon to help you release, shift, feel you reliance, and ultimately transform.

STEP 1:
Find Stillness This step is all about creating space for inner reflection. Find a quiet spot where you feel comfortable and won't be disturbed. Take several deep breaths, allowing your body to relax and your mind to calm. This stillness opens you up to receive insights and guidance.

1. In this moment of stillness, what thoughts or feelings arise? What is your inner voice trying to tell you?

_____

_____

_____

_____

_____

_____

_____

_____

_____

_____

_____

_____

_____

_____

_____

_____

TAURUS PRACTICES

STEP 2:

Connect with your body As you tune into your physical self, notice any sensations of resistance or anxiety. These bodily responses are natural as we prepare for change.

2. Where in your body do you feel resistance to change? How can you work with these sensations rather than against them?

_____

_____

_____

_____

_____

_____

_____

_____

_____

_____

_____

_____

_____

_____

_____

_____

_____

TAURUS PRACTICES

List your self-sabotaging patterns. Consider how these patterns might be walls you've built to keep yourself in your comfort zone. They may have once served you, but now they're limiting your growth.

3. What self-imposed walls have you created that keep you in your comfort zone? How have these walls blocked me from attracting new energies and experiences?

_____

_____

_____

_____

_____

_____

_____

_____

_____

_____

_____

_____

_____

_____

_____

_____

_____

_____

_____

_____

TAURUS PRACTICES

STEP 4:

Visualize your comfort zones. Your comfort zone is like a cozy, familiar room. It's safe, it's predictable, and it requires little effort to exist there. But here's the thing - real magic happens when we step out of that room and into the unknown.

4. Visualize your comfort zone as a physical space. What does it look like? How does it feel? Now, imagine what lies beyond its borders. What possibilities can you see?

TAURUS PRACTICES

As you stand at the threshold between comfort and growth, you might feel a mix of excitement and fear. That's completely normal. In fact, it's a sign you're on the right track.

5. What does the edge of your comfort zone feel like in your body? Where do you feel excitement? Where do you feel fear? Can you welcome both sensations as guides on your journey?"

_____

_____

_____

_____

_____

_____

_____

_____

_____

_____

_____

_____

_____

_____

_____

_____

_____

_____

_____

_____

_____

_____

_____

_____

TAURUS PRACTICES

STEP 5:

Embrace discomfort. Growth isn't always comfortable, but it's always worthwhile. When we push ourselves to try new things, we're literally rewiring our brains and expanding our potential.

6. Think of a time when you pushed through discomfort and grew as a result. How did it feel during the process? How did you feel afterwards? What did you learn about yourself?

_____

_____

_____

_____

_____

_____

_____

_____

_____

_____

_____

_____

_____

_____

_____

_____

_____

_____

_____

_____

_____

_____

_____

_____

_____

TAURUS PRACTICES

Taurus energy encourages us to find stability and appreciate what we have, while Scorpio pushes us to transform and evolve. This Full Moon is about finding the balance between these energies.

7. How can you honor both your need for stability and your desire for growth? What would it look like to create a stable foundation that supports your evolution?

_____

_____

_____

_____

_____

_____

_____

_____

_____

_____

_____

_____

_____

_____

_____

_____

_____

_____

_____

_____

_____

_____

_____

_____

_____

TAURUS PRACTICES

Both Taurus and Scorpio also remind us of the power of presence. When we're fully present, we can navigate change with grace and learn from every experience.

Remember, growth isn't about pushing yourself to the breaking point. It's about finding that sweet spot where you're challenged enough to evolve, but not so much that you're overwhelmed.

Also, Growth isn't linear. There will be times of rapid expansion and times of integration and rest. Both are equally important.

8. How can you honor both the active and restful phases of your growth journey? What would it look like to fully embrace wherever you are in the cycle?

TAURUS PRACTICES

As you work with this Full Moon energy, remember that you're not just changing - you're revealing more of your true self. Every step you take outside your comfort zone is a step towards embodying more of your innate power and potential.

What's one bold step you can take during this Full Moon cycle to expand your comfort zone? How will you celebrate your courage in taking this step?

Remember, you have the strength and wisdom within you to navigate this growth journey. Trust yourself, listen to your intuition, and keep moving forward, one brave step at a time.

_____

_____

_____

_____

_____

_____

_____

_____

_____

_____

_____

_____

_____

_____

_____

_____

_____

_____

_____

_____

_____

_____

_____

_____

_____

LAST QUARTER IN VIRGO

NOVEMBER 22ND

The Sun has transitioned from Scorpio to Sagittarius, where it now squares the Moon in Virgo and brings us our last Quarter Moon. This marks the final phase of the lunar cycle before we return to the New Moon. The last Quarter Moon gives us an opportunity for a final release of energies before we craft new intentions at the start of the next lunar cycle. Occasionally, these energies resist the release, and it feels like we are stuck with them. Stagnant energies can make us feel tense, irritable, or restless. If you are feeling any of these ways today, ask yourself what you are resisting. What energy are you holding on to that needs to leave your field or be transmuted in some way?

This last Quarter Moon is themed by the sign of the goddess, Virgo. Virgo is a great healer of the zodiac and often illuminates places where we need love, acceptance, and nourishment in our lives. Virgo reminds us that we have a unique gift to give this world and that our job is to feel worthy of it. We need to feel good enough to give our offering to others and show up for both ourselves and the world. This feeling of self-worth requires that we lay down any need for perfection and accept ourselves.

As you work with the energy of this last Quarter Moon, feel into the Earth element supporting you. Look to the Earth for inspiration. She is perfectly imperfect, and so are you. Flowers do not fail to shine because their petals are uneven. A tree does not fail to stand tall because its branches are crooked. No one looks at the Moon and thinks it is not good enough because it is only partially lit. We honor and celebrate nature's imperfections. Honor and celebrate your own imperfections this night and know that you deserve just as much appreciation for your beauty as the Earth, the Moon, and all the stars do.

With tonight's Moon in Virgo, you are asked to heal the part of yourself that does not feel worthy of your journey. What makes you feel not good enough for your dreams and visions? What part needs healing, love, and nurturing for you to grasp your potential? And are there any resistances within your energy that prevent you from fully releasing energies that no longer serve you? Any resistance will initially feel like frustration. Breathe into it and know that everything passes. Give yourself compassion and love. This energy will heal you and shift your energy in the direction of your true power.

What are you willing to let go this Last Quarter Moon to allow yourself to receive new energy?

AFFIRMATIONS

Describe the beauty of nature in a few statements or words. Think about the trees, sky, ocean, and other bodies of water around you and describe them. Create a free-flowing list of all the things you admire about nature. You can even include the stars, the Moon, and the Sun as part of your list as we experience them on Earth as well.

_____

_____

_____

_____

_____

_____

_____

_____

_____

_____

Next, create 3-5 statements or mantras for yourself that draw on the qualities listed above. Write down powerful "I am" statements that align you with the beauty of nature. For instance, if you wrote "powerful" or "resilient," create a mantra that states, "I am powerful and resilient in the face of obstacles" or something along those lines. Be creative with these and let them remind you that you are part of the Earth, and she is part of you.

_____

_____

_____

_____

_____

_____

_____

_____

_____

_____

_____

HAPPY
FULL MOON!

Thank you to everyone who supported and purchased this workbook.

Special Thanks to Rebecca Reitz (rebeccareitz.com, @becca_reitz) for her beautiful artwork on the cover & pages 2, 4, 10, 12, 16, 20, & 32.

For a monthly subscription contact hello@spiritdaughter.com or visit www.spiritdaughter.com.

Follow along our journey on IG:
@spiritdaughter

We always love seeing your photos & hearing about your experiences with the workbooks! Tag us to be featured on our community page:
@spiritdaughtercollective